3/12/93

How the Ox Star Fell from Heaven

How the Ox Star Fell from Heaven

ALBERT WHITMAN & COMPANY • Morton Grove, Illinois

Retold and illustrated by **LILY TOY HONG**

In the beginning, oxen did not live on earth.
They could only be found in the heavens, among the stars.
They lived with the Emperor of All the Heavens
in his Imperial Palace.

Clothed in robes of the finest silk, they reclined on billowy clouds. They never had to work, and their lives were easy.

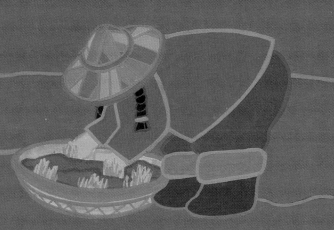

Life on earth was hard,
especially hard since oxen
did not live here. Farmers
had no beast of burden
to help with the planting
of vegetables and rice
in the spring

or with the gathering of crops at harvest time.

People were always tired and hungry. They labored from sunup to sundown, yet they could never finish all their work. Because there was so little food, they sometimes went three, four, even five days without one single meal.

But the Emperor of All the Heavens had not forgotten the earth. He knew that the poor peasants worked long and hard, and he believed that they should be able to eat every third day. With this in mind, he issued a decree: "The people of earth shall eat at least once every three days!"

He called upon his most trusted messenger,
the Ox Star, to deliver the message. Dressed
in a magnificent silk robe and a golden crown,
the Ox Star set off on the long and lonely
journey down to earth.

When he arrived, all the peasants hurried out to meet him. "I come with a message from the Emperor of All the Heavens," he bellowed. But the Ox Star, while strong, was not very smart. He twisted the Emperor's words: "The Emperor has declared that you shall eat three times a day, every day!" The peasants cheered and cheered.

The Emperor of All the Heavens heard his messenger's mistake and was angry. When the Ox Star arrived back at the Imperial Palace, he found the gates were locked. His princely robe and royal crown vanished. "Since you have betrayed my trust," the Emperor roared, "you shall never again be allowed in the heavens." The sky filled with lightning and thunder, and the Ox Star wept.

Suddenly everything turned dark. In a whirlwind,
the Ox Star was hurled through the stormy sky.
Down, down, down to earth he fell.

From that day, the Ox Star became a beast of burden, helping farmers. Around his thick neck he wore a heavy yoke, and through his nose he wore a ring.

The other oxen were sent to earth, too. They labored day after day in the fields, pulling plows through the ground at planting time and helping to gather the crops at harvest time.

Today, because of the Ox Star's ill fortune and his careless mistake, a bit of heaven remains on earth. For those who have an ox, good soil, and enough rain, life is not as hard as it once was. Best of all, they can eat warm rice, tender vegetables, and Chinese sweet cakes three times a day, every day!

Now when you look up at the night sky, so beautiful and bright, think of the Ox Star, who fell from the heavens, and of his blunder, which became a blessing.

For my parents

Library of Congress Cataloging-in-Publication Data

Hong, Lily Toy.
How the ox star fell from heaven/
retold and illustrated by Lily Toy Hong.
p. cm.
Summary: A Chinese folk tale which explains why
the ox was banished from heaven to become the
farmer's beast of burden.
ISBN 0-8075-3428-5
[1. Folklore—China.] I. Title.
  PZ8.1.H755Ho 1991   90-38978
398.24′5297358′0951—dc20   CIP   AC

Text and illustrations © 1991 by Lily Toy Hong.
Published in 1991 by Albert Whitman & Company,
6340 Oakton Street, Morton Grove, Illinois 60053.
Published simultaneously in Canada
by General Publishing, Limited, Toronto.
All rights reserved. Printed in the U.S.A.
10 9 8 7 6 5 4 3 2 1

Typography by Karen Johnson Campbell.
The text typeface is Fritz Quadrata.
The illustrations were done in
airbrushed acrylics and gouache.

LILY TOY HONG

Lily Toy Hong has lived most of her life in Salt Lake City, Utah. She grew up in a large Chinese-American family, the seventh of nine children, and says she always knew she wanted to write and illustrate children's books when she grew up.

After studying art at Utah Technical College and Utah State University, she worked for three years as an illustrator for a greeting-card company before becoming a freelance designer and illustrator. *How the Ox Star Fell from Heaven* is her first published book.

Lily got the idea for this picture book after she did an illustration of oxen for a college art assignment on water. Later, when she discovered the folktale on which the story is based, she expanded the illustration into a picture book. The final illustrations were done in gouache and airbrushed acrylics.

Besides working on her art, Lily enjoys learning more about Chinese culture and eating rice every day.